AN ODYSSEY OF SELF-DISCOVERY

OKUHLE ESETHU

OE PUBLICATIONS

First published in South Africa in 2024 by

OE Publications

Copyright © Lindokuhle Esethu Hlatshwayo, 2024

All rights reserved.

This text or any portion thereof may not be reproduced or used in any manner whatsoever without the prior written permission of both the copyright owner and the publisher of this book.

ISBN: 978-1-0370-0257-1

For more information visit: www.oepublications.com

losing Self

...

searching for Self

...

returning to Self

a body evolving

sometimes
you forget your own body

you move at a slow pace
because
you are tired
of being a being

then it outgrows you

leaves you behind

forgets that you are only human

it evolves

and exists
outside of you

Okuhle Esethu

far far away
from you

it becomes
a distant figure

a distant figure

engulfed by grief, of Self,
she began to exist as an elusive visage
of herself.

she suffered from the sickness
that never goes away.
the kind that makes the soul nauseous.

phantom existence

what happens when my own existence
becomes a burden to me?

what happens when i become unaware
of my own existence?

what happens when i exist
with no record of
who i am,
why i am here,
where i will go from here?

what happens when my own existence
feels like
a phantom dream,
a distant memory,
an intangible and elusive force in nature?

elusive

she became elusive
to herself
in her last days
as herself...

something was lost—
a part of her soul,
a shadow of her being,
a layer of her mind.

her eyes became vacant,
like no one lived inside
her hollow body anymore,
as she receded into the darkness.

the loss was too ferocious;
it fractured the feeble fragments of her frame.
she existed as a fleeting memory.

mist

i am an elusive figure
on this earth.
my very existence
is ephemeral.

like the mist,
my sense of Self
disappears ever,
burdening me
with this existential void.

a life devoid of meaning

a life

devoid

of meaning

only creates

a void

that one cannot avoid.

un-alive

i am numb.
i am drained of energy.
i am un-alive.

out of body experiences

i observed my body fall into deep sleep.
i died for a while.
i existed outside of my body.
it no longer belonged to me.
it became a stranger.

who am i

am i my past?
who i used to be?
who i was told and taught to be?
what happened to me?

am i my present?
who i think i should be?
who i feel like right now?
what i am being right now?

am i my future?
who i dream of becoming?
who i could become?
what i idealise?

façades

strip away the façade
built from papier-mâché
of your material wealth,
and you reveal
a breathing yet lifeless being,
an empty soul.

the earthly possessions
that define you
are illusions
deluding you
and making the real you
elude you.

you are nothing.
you are no one.

flames of suffering

a vicious fire of truth
has scorched the illusion of
who i imagined i am
and left me
with only the remnants of
my former Self.

i live as a shadow of myself.

i do not know who i am.
i do not know what i am on this earth.
i do not know why i am on this earth.

who can endure the flames of suffering
and still be the same?

tides of selfhood

***going against the tides of your identity

the Self
is easily shattered
under the weight of betrayal

leaving a split facade
that you cannot face
that you cannot live with

the Self is fragile

a spiritual being

you spend so much time

worrying

about the flesh

when the soul is starved.

ego

a bullet of truth to the heart

and the ego dies

all of its noisy thoughts
negative energies
and insecurities

subside

…

noise of the ego

it's not only the outside world
that has silenced me,
but also this inner voice.

it's not only the outside world
that i've had to silence,
but also this inner voice.

this voice
drowned me
whenever i shut my eyes.

the noise
of the ego
is excruciating.

                              there's some
                              existential weight
                              to being a human being.

humanness

the ego
cannot survive
in the ocean of humanity.

one who does not yet know themself
cannot tolerate another.

one who does not yet love themself
is filled with hatred.

the ego
drowns
in the ocean of humility.

survival

it is a lot harder surviving
when you have nothing to live for.

what it means to be alive

to be human.
to be breathing.
to be struggling for life
while the hands of time
grow grey hairs on your head,
mark more memories in your mind,
turn your heart into stone,
and make your body a womb then a tomb.

to be moving closer
to your last breath with each breath.

in another realm

in another realm,
i am better than this—

i am myself.
i am my highest Self.
i've reached my peak potential.
i've self-actualised.
i've become all i could possibly be.

in this realm,
i am just existing.

nothing is as meaningless as life

i'd like to die, sooner.

i think death is sweeter
when you have not lived for too long—
scarred
and
marred
into a traumatised being—
only to die in the end,
for nothing.

nothing is as meaningless as life.

an urgent funeral

burn me
at midnight
after i've taken my last breath
at night.

let me say my goodbyes
at dawn
be coiled with the dust
sooner.

do not prolong my death
till dusk.
do not let my loved ones suffer too long,
seeing and smelling my corpse.

**grieving loss of Self.

gnawing grief

where to put all this grief...

anywhere else but here

it's too heavy for my frail body.
it's too burdensome for my fractured heart.

Okuhle Esethu

navigating trauma

with no words
to articulate
my anguish

with no memories
to recall
ways of healing

with no guide
to navigate
through the labyrinth of my trauma

my sense of Self diminished day by day
until i was nothing
but a wounded soul

bruises

"who do you weep for?"

my inner child.
the one who was hurt,
who is hurting,
who carries hurt and hatred in her heart
and doesn't even know it.

grieving

they cry for their past Selves
so much
that their bones bleed

the blood spills onto the ground
the spot where they grow seeds of hope

the blood spoils the seeds with despair

despair that further separates them
from themselves

despair that keeps their hauntings alive

despair that holds them in bondage

despair that keeps the past alive
and their souls drained of life

the right to grieve

grief is a response to loss.

there are many things that one can lose
in this life:
loss of purpose.
loss of passion.
loss of Self.
loss of the desire to dream, to live.

one has the right to grieve
what is lost.
one is not only limited to grieving
because of death.

everything that has meaning
is worth
grieving for.

bones ache

much has happened

…and when you cannot go any further, rest!

healing old wounds

do not build an altar for your trauma.
do not worship your pain.

heal.

heal the wounds of your past.
the ones no one dares to focus on.
the ones that are not considered traumatic
but actually cut deep and fracture the heart.

healing through words

every night,
after battling with the world's brutalities,
she sits down to write,
letting her pain pour
from the pores of her bruised heart
to pen
to paper.

words soothe her wounds,
it seems.

poetry allows her to erase her traumas
and rewrite herself,
she says.

she doesn't want to exist
as a bruised woman.

she'd rather live
with a body saturated with unfinished poems.

poems

yesterday, i woke up with a poem in my heart.
i wish i had written it down
before it escaped my body
and got swept away by the winds of chaos.

today, i woke up with a weary body
and a wretched heart, empty of poems.
it's impossible being a poet
when you are trying to survive.

tomorrow, i may wish to die.
i will die with a burdened heart
and a body filled with regret
for all the poems not written.

…

chaos

i do not have any poems inside me tonight.

it's all silence.
emptiness.
darkness.
a void of nothingness.

warfare

life has cast me into a warfare.
it is only poetry that is keeping me alive.
i've used it as a sword.
i've used it as a shield.
i've used it as a light
in the darkness of the night,
when my soul's lustre was dimmed,
when my own mind turned into an enemy.

life has cast me into a warfare.
my body is a battlefield.
my body is a battlefield.
my body is a battlefield.
my body is a battlefield.
my body is a battlefield.
it is only poetry that is keeping my bones
from breaking and withering away.

dark alley

{in a dark alley}

i've had to set myself on fire
to light a path for myself
to find my way back home

now that i've sacrificed myself
for myself
i do not know who i am

i've lost myself
in the ashes and smoke
and darkness

with no mirrors
to reflect back to me
who i am

a mirror to my wounds

i thought i knew myself
until you put a mirror before me.

a mirror
that reflected my true nature.
a mirror
that revealed my darkest secrets.
a mirror
that portrayed me as a villain in my own story.

now that i cannot live with myself,
because you put a mirror before me,
who is to blame for my suicide?

lost, too

my lover

his demeanour exudes self-disdain.
his lack of self-worth is unmistakable.
he asks me to save him from himself,
to help him find himself.

i tell him
i've lost myself, too.

my light has been dimmed
by the darkness of my past—
the hurt, the lies, the betrayal.

i have no torch
to search for other human beings,
to light them up,
to help them find themselves.

i have to find myself, first.

what does it mean to be lost

to have a name
yet be without history.
to be detached
from your people.
to be searching for a home endlessly
because you have been displaced
from the land connected
to your umbilical cord.
to look at your reflection
but not see your true Self.
to not know who you are.
to gag on clan names
that are too powerful
for your softened tongue.
to not remember home.
to not remember your history.
to not remember your people.
to not remember who you were
before they told you who you should be.
to be a shallow shell of yourself…

home

home is only a good place to visit,
not to live there forever.

otherwise, it binds you,
forces you to remain the same person—
who you always were,
who you were told to be.

with no roots

she has no stories to tell
about herself—
who she is
where she comes from
what she wishes to become—
because she has no history.

her story is phantom.

with no roots,
she fades away
with dust,
easily blown away
by the winds and waves of life.

memories of the past

my past remembers me
more than i remember it.

i've mastered closing off
my traumatic memories.

but.
when i am alone
i am haunted by the skeletons of my sins.
my mind forces me to sift through my old life
to recall emotionally damaging experiences that leave
the air vibrating with sadness.

without a history

without a history,
the Self is a momentary phenomenon—

a being existing as different Selves
in a lifetime.
each Self coming into existence
and ceasing to exist
with passing time.

**the Self is limited to time,
identifying with an experience
and dying when that experience ends.

the scars of history

history repeats itself
when you don't heal.

        ignored weals
        open up and become wounds.
        old wounds become irksome scars.

history repeats itself
when you don't heal.

                spin itches
                from the scars
                etched
                by the brutality of the past
                on your back.

history hurts
when you don't rewrite it.

yesterday

you bleed yesterday's tears into a new day.
dawn has come
yet
you still let the shadows of your past
haunt you

the scars of your history
itch your heart

you have no one
to scratch the pain away

you have no one to hold you
while you grieve
your past Self

do not turn to yesterday for comfort

turn to yourself

fragmented self

when there is a disconnect
between
the past and the present,
the Self
dissipates
from the realm of consciousness,
into the unknown.

the Self
becomes displaced
from their inner world.

this estrangement is marked by
fading memories and fleeting dreams.

timelessness

time.   eludes.   me.

the
    uncountable hours
evaporate into seconds,
threatening the essence
of my being, my life…

time floats
around me like the wind.
it gloats
about its elusive nature.

when i try to
catch up with it,
clasp onto it,
contain it,
contract it,
it flees with the wind,
flirting with every force of nature
that threatens to erase my existence.

losing self

whenever you feel lost.
whenever you feel like you do not know
who you are anymore.
whenever you feel detached from yourself.
return to your home.
return to your core.
return to the birthplace of the Self.
let the beginning of your life
guide you back to Self.

...

silent echoes

when your soul
feels burdened
by your shallowness

when your soul
is sickened
by living in a hollow shell of a being
instead of a lively body

when your soul
gives up
pretending to be content
with a half-lived life

            it will call to you
            to return to your true Self
            to remember who you are
            to redefine yourself

Okuhle Esethu

        it will urge you
        to choose what lights you up

        it will compel you
        to live
        not merely exist

when your soul
finally refuses
to be intertwined
with a self-estranged being

        it will beckon you
        to reconnect with yourself

the silence of the morning

i miss the silence of the morning…

when peace seems eternal.
when my existence is intertwined with
the soul of the universe.

silence the world

lose yourself in the   s i l e n c e

illuminate the darkness
of your lost soul with peacefulness

the soul needs nurturing
the soul needs tending to like a garden
the soul needs to be soothed with silence

lost in the abyss

the silence
may be overpowering
when you have not honed
your inner voice.

you may drown
in the silence
when you do not know yourself.

you may get lost
in the gaping abyss of the silence
when you do not trust your intuition.

…

                                  find yourself…
                                            find yourself…

darkness

slide into the darkest crevices of your soul.
there, you may discover a way
to light up
yourself.

a light that will make
silence
easier to exist in.

slide into the darkest crevices of your soul.
there, you may discover a way
to embrace
your complexities and imperfections.

one has to be able to live
within themselves,
to be content with their existence.

a shapeless shadow

the Self
is
an undefinable form

a shapeless shadow

why do you exist

to try and figure out
the purpose and meaning
of existence.

—i think.

who you are

who
you
believe
you are
is a story
you
continuously
tell and retell.

storytelling self

we tell ourselves
and others
stories
about ourselves,
which create
narratives of the Self.

thus,
the existence of the Self
is only a biographic fiction.

a repeated story
internalised to dictate our lives—
who
we show up in the world as.

personhood

it is your pattern
of
thoughts, feelings, and ways of being
that make you you.

it is the continuously
preached and practiced
idea of who you are
that makes up your personality.

this is not who you are

reduce the noise of the ego
to hear the whispers of your higher Self,
which has been silenced
ever since
you forgot how to be yourself
in this ugly world.

questions

the knowledge that you seek
to self-actualise
and connect with your higher Self
is already within.

death of self

allow the old you to die
so you may be reborn.

the death of Self
is necessary for you to evolve.

you cannot remain the same forever.

void

of course,
there'll be a gaping void
left
when you outgrow
the old, decayed parts of your being—

a merciless abyss
that swallows you whole
and leaves you
feeling empty and helpless.

that's the nature
of shedding old skin
and familiarising yourself
with a different version of yourself.

at first,
the new
is scary,
it's a stranger,
until it becomes you and you become it.

pus

muscles ache
when you don't move.
the body grows blisters
and oozes pus
when you are not growing.

you are not meant to rot away your existence.
the Self is meant to evolve with time.

__time__

you cannot tell time what it should be.

time is like fairy dust;
it sparkles and shimmers
with a magical and ethereal glow.

time can be blurry,
like a misty dream.

time is elusive.

no one can define time.
no one can control time.
no one can change the power time
has over our reality.
no one can predict the influence of time
on who we become.

the boundaries
we set for ourselves
against time
dissolve
when we accept
time's true essence.

we become free to exist
as our best Selves
when we realise that time just is,
and we should let it be.

ephemeral

the Self
is a series of fleeting moments…

an ephemeral being.

you cannot define what fades…

the point of it all

life

is less about feelings

                                                (feelings are erosive and fleeting)

and more about memories

memories

my memories
are

remnants of my past

recollections of who i've been

records from the archive of my life

                                        what i remember
                                            is who i am

evidence

our memories
are remnants
of
our existence—evidence that we've lived.

dual existence

the Self is
finite.

the Self is
infinite.

*with light and darkness intertwined.

in every being,
there exists
a split image—
the Self
and
its shadow.

cycles of life

silence!
listen to human existence
echoing in the distance.

songs of extinction
and re-generation
forming a new vibration.

where there was once a living organism,
now lies a corpse.
this is the complex, cynical cycle of life.

plant a seed

plant a seed

so new roots

may grow

where an old tree

which has chipped away at itself

and eroded out of existence

once stood

growth not betrayal

you
are
growing…
evolving…

your body
is
developing,
not betraying
you.

your body

honour your body.

you know its rhythm.
you know its pace.

do not move
when it wishes to rest.

do not sleep
when it wishes to dance.

respect this body by listening to it.

a battle

i am learning to treat my body
with the kindness
it deserves.

only gentleness
will help my body and i win this battle.

words kill words heal

she died
and resurrected herself, again,
through words.

...

a moment of silence

a moment of silence

to
breathe

to
cleanse the spirit

to
nurture the heart

to
still the mind

to
free the ego

to
release

Okuhle Esethu

to
search

to
discover

to
return to Self

to
be

moments

the moments i thought mattered,
they've passed.

the moments i thought didn't matter,
they've passed.

all i have is this moment right here,
and it's all that matters.

blank spaces

silence,
like blank spaces,
is an invitation
to create,
to wipe away the darkness
that vexes the soul.

it rains

just be still
and listen to the rain.

allow your heart to dance
to the songs it sings.

let it wash away the anxieties
clogged up in your system.

let it soothe your soul
and put your mind at ease.

be still
and listen to the rain.

inner whispers

nurture
and listen
to the quiet, inner whispers
of your soul.

reconnect with your inner world.

whispers of your soul

surrender yourself
to discover your true Self.

the ego has been a stumbling block
to reconnecting with your true Self.

you cannot discover yourself
amidst its endless and meaningless chatter.

quiet the noise of the ego.
listen to the whispers of your soul.

return to self

reconnect
with the silence of your soul.
your heart aches
for you
to return home,
to yourself.

the noise of the external world
has swallowed you up.
you are too consumed by its banalities.

you have forgotten yourself.
you do not know who you are anymore.
you have no time for yourself.

an odyssey of self-discovery

enter the unknown to reconnect with yourself

redefine yourself

go beyond yourself

dance with the universe

recreate yourself

exist in a way you never have before

compass

your heart is your compass,
a guide back to Self
when you are lost in the dark woods.

explore

explore the intricacies of your being.
surrender yourself
to the process of self-discovery.

what makes you human?

solitude

long periods of solitude and silence
become necessary
when all you've known is chaos,
and the outside noise
drowns
the whispers from within.

seek peace!

your soul starves for your love.

outside noise

you need quiet time.
you need time
away from the outer world.

you need to traverse your inner world
to rediscover who you are,
to redefine who you are,
without the interference of this insane world.

disconnect

spend some time away
from the routine
of who you are.

step away
from your
mundane Self.

exist in a way
you never have before.

reinvent yourself.
discover who you can be
when you are not clinging
to your senseless identity.

the alchemy of self

the life you experience
is a mirror of who you are.

your inner world
creates
your outer reality.

you cannot change your life experiences
without changing yourself.

to live a life you love,
to be happy with yourself,
recreate yourself.

midnight

everything becomes so clear
when the rest of the world is asleep.
everything within me comes alight
in the darkness of the night.

in nature's presence

i stayed still and silent for eternity
and felt a wave of serenity
cleansing my burdened body
and soothing my scarred soul.

stillness

i used to wonder why *ugogo*
would spend hours under our apricot tree
doing nothing, just sitting still.

now i realise that slowing down to watch life go by
while you remain still is a way of feeling alive
and experiencing a deeper connection to existence.

nature

be still
and observe
how nature interacts with itself.
how it exists in this world.

everything simply is.
life is perfect.

birdlife

look at how birds
flock
to beautifully cultivated
and quiet gardens.

where there is peace,
there is life.
where there is beauty,
there is life.

cultivate your inner life.
make it peaceful.
make it beautiful.
make it wonderful.

a garden

nourish your soul
so you may reconnect with yourself.

the soul wilts and withers
when not tended to.

you become alienated from yourself;
your soul becomes a stranger to you
when you cease taking care of yourself.

nourish your soul
so you may grow closer to yourself.

the soul flourishes, like a garden,
when tended to.

seasons

everything changes
with each season,
including the Self.

i am not the person i once was.
i am not where i once was.
i am defined by my growth,

brought about by the different,
ever-evolving seasons
that continuously shape and reshape me.

inner growth

time buries the true nature of a being.
time rots the core of the heart.
time betrays the spirit.

…

nonetheless

true inner growth
involves excavating
the buried parts of yourself.

true inner growth
is reconnecting
with your ancient Self.

evolving

sometimes,
we think
we are evolving,
but actually,
we are returning
to our ancient Selves.

an evolved being

once i have evolved,
i cannot go back to
who i once was.

uma sengiguqukile
angikwazi ukuphindela emuva
ngiphinde ngibe yinto ebengiyiyona.

searching

i was walking along lonely streets
with a deep void in my heart.

i was walking along lonely streets
with sin heavy on the soles of my feet.

i was walking along lonely streets
with my strained soul singing songs of sorrow.

i was walking along lonely streets
attempting to summon up the courage to live.

i was walking along lonely streets
searching for my lost Self.

…

i was walking along lonely streets
when i found God.

dear self

dear Self,
i've been searching for you…

although i still haven't found you,
i feel closer to you
than ever before.

faint traces of your shadow
emerge
in the distance
when i open my eyes.

discovering you
no longer
resembles the disillusionment of a mirage.

sunrise

we woke up
when the sun was still soft.

its gentle glow
shone
on our shivering bodies,
warming us,
embracing us,
renewing us for the life we desired.

we woke up
at sunrise as better versions of ourselves.

greatness

it is not enough
for me
to simply exist.

i intend to take up space,
to shake this earth to its knees,
so that when i exit,
they all know that
a great giant
lived through these times.

magic

the magic
within you
is waiting to be rekindled.

...

what matters

at the end of life
nothing matters

nothing at all

.

life!
it's all just a moment;
there's no need to worry so much.

the end

when you get to the end,
you should like who you are.

An Odyssey of Self-Discovery

*In this collection, poetry becomes a profound exploration
of what it means to be human—a journey through the
labyrinth of the mind and soul.
Each poem delves into the search for authenticity,
peeling back the layers of existence to reveal the deeper
elements that define who we are and what we become.*

*This book is both existential and introspective,
inviting readers to confront the shadows within and
to question the identities they hold dear.
It is a poetic odyssey that navigates the turbulence of
loss, the yearning for understanding,
and the eventual discovery of a truer Self.*

*As you turn each page, you find yourself immersed in a
world where words become mirrors, reflecting the
continuous process of becoming.
Here, the journey is as significant as the destination,
and the exploration of the Self is endless.*

ABOUT THE WRITER

Okuhle Esethu, legally known as Lindokuhle Esethu Hlatshwayo, is a multifaceted creative force acclaimed for her work as a writer, poet, storyteller, and performer. As the author of nine books, she leverages her independent publishing company, OE Publications, to not only showcase her literary achievements but also to advocate for her intellectual property.

Her work is deeply rooted in a passion for literature, and she brings a unique voice to the world of creative writing. She skilfully blends various artistic forms to create compelling narratives.
Her diverse talents extend beyond the page, making her a dynamic presence in the creative arts scene. Whether through the written word, performance, or visual storytelling, Okuhle Esethu continues to push the boundaries of creative expression.

OTHER BOOKS

- *Full Circle (Poetry & Prose)*

- *Horrors Of The Past (Short Stories)*

- *Ugh, Life! (Poetry)*

- *Lover Of Life (Affirmations & Notes To Self)*

- *Senseless Existence (Poetry)*

- *Love Letter For My Country (Poetry)*

- *She Is Living Poetry*

- *A Woman's Body (Prose, Monologues & Short Stories)*

By Okuhle Esethu

www.ingramcontent.com/pod-product-compliance
Lightning Source LLC
Chambersburg PA
CBHW070507100426
42743CB00010B/1787